HANDBALL

Richard C. Nelson
Harlan S. Berger

HANDBALL

Prentice-Hall, Inc., Englewood Cliffs, New Jersey

C-13-372441-7
P-13-372433-6

Library of Congress Catalog Card Number 74-149311

Printed in the United States of America

Current Printing (last digit):

12   11   10   9   8   7   6   5   4   3   2

PRENTICE-HALL INTERNATIONAL, INC., London
PRENTICE-HALL OF AUSTRALIA, PTY. LTD., Sydney
PRENTICE-HALL OF CANADA, LTD., Toronto
PRENTICE-HALL OF INDIA PRIVATE LIMITED, New Delhi
PRENTICE—HALL OF JAPAN, INC., Tokyo

CONTENTS

v

HANDBALL

I

The
First
Step

1

WHAT YOU NEED
TO PLAY HANDBALL

This chapter concerns:
1. What physical and emotional qualities you need
to play handball
2. What factors might prevent you from playing
3. What clothing and equipment you will need

PERSONAL NEEDS, BENEFITS, AND ATTRACTIONS

The few physical attributes needed to play handball are mobility, flexibility, and cardio-respiratory endurance. The handball player does not need great physical or muscular strength.

In this sport of fast reflexes and sudden stops and starts, an individual of average build and strength has more than an even break when competing with a taller, heavier man because much of the action takes place near the floor. The shorter man does not have to move as far to reach the ball and therefore is better able to develop the proper stroke.

In addition, since four-wall handball is played in a confined space and since each man tries to hit the ball against a wall in such a way that the other man cannot return it, the action is fast and furious. The small playing area and the high volleying rate force players to change direction quickly and frequently, necessitating rapid total body movements as well as equally fast limb movements. People with shorter limbs can usually start, stop, and change direction faster than a taller, heavier man. In part, this explains why an average or small man can more than hold his own on a handball court.

Psychologically, the handball player needs patience and self-reliance, especially in a game of singles (one against one). He also needs an analytical mind: successful play demands a constant analysis of the opponent's style and strategy and the ability to change one's own attack to counteract that of the opponent.

In doubles play, each man must be aware of his partner's mental attributes and physical skills as well as those of his opponents and play accordingly. Doubles play is more complex, and some players have to work hard to stifle their normal aggressive tendency to go after every shot as they would in singles.

There are two main handicaps which might prevent a man from playing handball, or at least from developing his skill to the point where he could enjoy the game: extreme height and weight. Extreme height can severely restrict mobility, and extra weight can put a man completely at the mercy of a much smaller but more agile player. Because so much agility and stamina are necessary, the greatly overweight person should probably not play. The only other handicap preventing play is poor eyesight. People whose eyesight can be improved sufficiently by eyeglasses or contact lenses may play, but they should wear unbreakable glasses or an eye guard. There are, however, people with one or more of the preceding handicaps who play, and some have compensated to the point where they do quite well.

People are attracted to handball for many reasons. In addition to the fact that smallness poses no handicap, many people like handball because of the necessity and challenge of developing the weak or offhand. The natural right hander must learn to hit with his left; the southpaw, with his right. Handball is also an efficient and delightful way to condition the body and maintain a high level of physical fitness. In addition, the competition and the rapid, continuous pace provide a beneficial change in thought from business and everyday problems. In a nutshell, physical fitness and the chance for mental relaxation are the two main benefits of handball.

However, there are other attractions. For one, the game is simple. Each man tries to hit a rubber ball against the front wall of a box-like court so as to make it impossible for his opponent to return the ball to the same wall. One man serves; if the other returns the ball to the front wall they volley alternately until one or the other cannot return the ball. Only the server can score points; it takes 21 points to win a game.

Other attractions include simple, quickly learned rules, inexpensive equipment and clothing, and the opportunity to fraternize and find new friends on the courts. Include the low-risk nature of the sport—the possibility of injury is relatively slight compared to other sports—and it is clear why the popularity of handball is rising and why it is called a lifetime sport.

CLOTHING, EQUIPMENT, AND FACILITIES

The required clothing and equipment are simple and inexpensive. The clothing worn by handball players comprises a loose-fitting pair of gym shorts, a short-sleeved gym shirt, an athletic supporter, a pair of thick sweat socks, comfortable gym shoes, and snug-fitting handball gloves. If eyeglasses are necessary, they should be unbreakable. Elastic retainers, or some other device, must be worn to secure the glasses during fast stops and starts. For those who do not wear glasses or who wear contact lenses, wire or plastic eye guards are available to protect against injury.

The gym shorts and shirt must fit loosely to allow for stretching and bending. The shirt should be heavy enough to soak up considerable perspiration—a sweat-spotted floor can cause slipping and sliding. Clothing should be light in color, preferably white (the only color allowed in tournament play).

Gloves are mandatory. They protect the hands and keep the ball dry. Beginners should use the thicker, padded gloves until their hands toughen and then switch to the thinner, unpadded gloves for better ball control.

All gloves must fit tightly. The better gloves have wrist tabs that stick together on contact to provide a more convenient method of fastening the gloves as well as a firmer fit compared with the buckle-and-strap gloves.

Gym shoes should also fit snugly; blisters and worn out socks and shoes result from a loose fit. To prevent these problems, many players wear two pairs of socks. Low-quarter shoes are most commonly worn. The best ones that can be bought are usually the bargain, for the fast stops and starts quickly ruin poorly made shoes.

Two other items are necessary to play. One is a ball; the other, a court. The standard ball weighs 2.3 ounces, is $1\frac{7}{8}$ inches in diameter, and is made of black rubber. The standard four-wall court is 40' long and 20' wide with a 20' ceiling (see Fig. 1-1). The court is split in half by the short line; paralleling the short line and five feet in front of it is the service line. The two service boxes, 18" wide between the court and service lines at either side of the court, accommodate the partner not serving in a doubles game.

Unfortunately, not all courts are a standard size. Worse, there are not enough courts. Robert Kendler, president of the United States Handball Association, said in 1969, "If anything casts a shadow on handball, it's the lack of courts. We're 100,000 courts behind." But more courts are being built, most

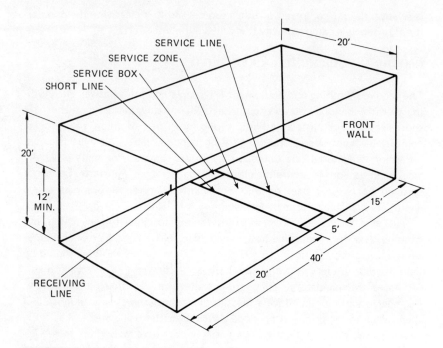

FIGURE 1-1. Standard four-wall court dimensions

of them at YMCAs, athletic clubs, and universities and colleges. In addition, many of the newer courts are being built with galleries to accommodate spectators, a measure of the increasing popularity of the game.

AFTER READING THIS CHAPTER, YOU SHOULD KNOW THAT:

People of average or smaller build can learn to play handball well.

Psychologically, very little distinguishes a good handball player from any other athlete.

Extreme height and poor eyesight hamper development of handball skills. Extremely overweight individuals should not play.

Special gloves, socks, shoes, trunks, shirt, and athletic supporter constitute the necessary clothing. Some kind of eye protection is also recommended.

Four-wall handball is played in a 40′ X 20′ X 20′ court.

2

PLAYING THE GAME

Primarily, this chapter covers:
1. The rules of the game and basic strategy
2. How to hit the ball and the basic serves
and shots employed
3. Safety factors

RULES

Two, three, or four persons can play handball in singles, cut-throat, or doubles whether the game be one, three, or four wall. Singles is a stern test of stamina, exposing mistakes and weaknesses quickly. Three men rotate in cutthroat, the server playing the other two. Doubles pits two against two and emphasizes teamwork. No matter which version of the game is played, the rules are much the same. Only one hand at a time may be used to hit the ball. The ball must be hit; it may not be caught or slung.

Let us first consider the singles game. Before the game begins, you must determine which player is to serve first. In tournament play, a coin is tossed. In informal play, the ball is often thrown against the front wall. The player whose rebound comes closest to the short line wins the serve. The server may stand anywhere he wishes in the service zone (between the short and service lines). He then drops or bounces the ball on the floor; the ball may bounce no more than three times before it must be hit. The ball must hit the front wall before hitting the side wall, ceiling, or floor. If it does not, the server loses the serve. This loss of serve, called a handout, also occurs if the ball touches the server anywhere except his hand during the act of serving or if it strikes him after rebounding from the front wall.

There are other nonplayable serves; they are called fault serves. If the server hits a fault serve, he has one more opportunity to serve. However, any two of the following four fault serves constitute a handout.

Short, two-side, ceiling, and long are the four fault serves (see Figs. 2-1 and 2-2). The short serve does not carry over the short line (see Fig. 1-1). Two-side serves strike both side walls before contacting the floor. Long serves carry to the back wall or to one side wall and the back wall before touching

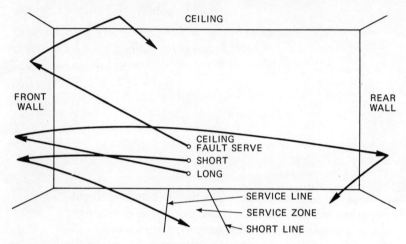

FIGURE 2-1. Fault serves not involving side walls (side view of court)

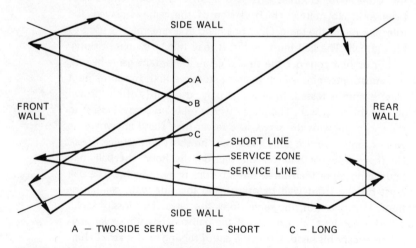

FIGURE 2-2. Fault serves involving side walls (top view of court)

the floor. The ceiling serve touches the ceiling after rebounding from the front wall.

The server may not step on or outside the short or service lines during the serve. If he does so, he is guilty of a foot fault. Two foot faults in a row or one foot fault and a fault serve constitute a handout.

The server may not use his body to block the receiver's view of the ball during the serve. This "screen ball" is replayed as a hinder (the meaning of this term will be explained shortly).

Before the serve, the receiver must stand at least five feet behind the short line (behind the receiving line marked on the side wall). After the server hits the ball, the receiver may move forward only as far as the short line to return the serve. If his forward motion carries him into the service zone, the server automatically receives a point.

After a legal serve (after the ball contacts the front wall and rebounds to the floor in back of the short line—see Figs. 2-3, 2-4, and 2-5) the receiver must hit the ball before it strikes the floor again; or, should the serve be high enough, he may elect to hit it in the air. Whether he hits it on the first bounce or on the fly, the ball must carry to the front wall before it again strikes the floor. If the receiver cleanly misses the served ball (an ace) or hits it so weakly that it touches the floor before hitting the front wall, the server wins the point.

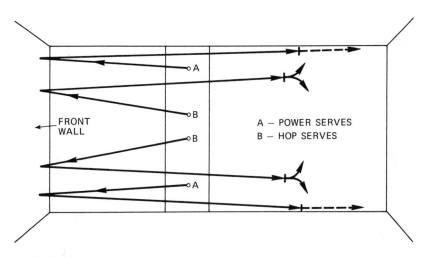

FIGURE 2-3. Legal power and hop serves (top view of court)

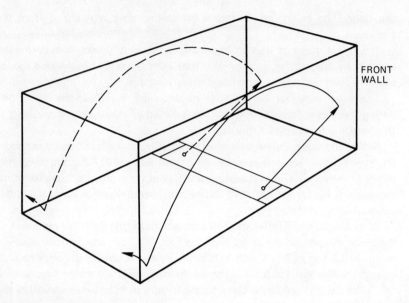

FIGURE 2-4. Legal lob serves

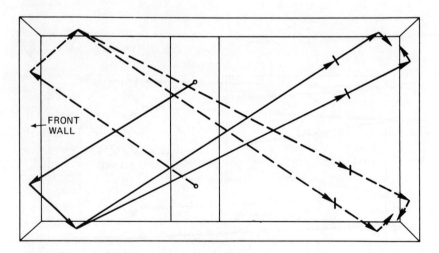

FIGURE 2-5. Legal Z serves (angle or scotch toss) (top view of court)

If the receiver successfully returns the serve to the front wall, the rebound becomes the responsibility of the server. After the initial serve, any returned ball may rebound off any combination of side or back walls and ceiling before touching the front wall. The players continue to hit the ball alternately until a shot fails to reach the front wall. If the receiver fails, the server gains a point. If the server cannot return the shot, a handout results and the serve passes to the receiver.

Hinders may happen during volleying or during a serve in the form of a screen ball. In play, when one player unavoidably blocks another, either physically or visually, from making his shot, the person hindered should so indicate and his opponent should honor the call. There is no loss of serve or change of score on a hinder. The hinder rule should be observed scrupulously since good handball play hinges on the right of each man to a clear, unobstructed shot at the ball.

Sometimes the ball hits a player. If a player's shot strikes an opponent, the volley is taken over with no change in score or service, no matter what direction the ball takes after contact. However, if a player hits himself with his own shot or strikes his partner, the opposition receives a point or the service, depending on who originally served the ball.

Some practices are as much a courtesy as a rule during informal play; in tournament play, whether these practices have been violated is decided by the referee. For example, gloves wet enough to cause erratic behavior of the ball should not be worn. Each player should have extra pairs of gloves and change whenever necessary.

Wrist shots are prohibited and should be called immediately by the offending player. Such shots invoke the penalty of a point for the other player or loss of serve.

If a player dives for a low shot or otherwise attempts to return a low shot in such a way that neither man is certain if the player actually returned the ball on the first bounce, this volley should be replayed, as should any involving uncertainty or dispute.

A point or loss of serve is assessed against any player deliberately delaying the game for longer than ten seconds. Only three time outs of 30 seconds each are allowed per game per singles player or doubles team.

Rules for doubles follow those for singles. One player stands in a service box while his partner serves. In each game, only one handout is permitted the team serving first; that is, after the initial server's serve is broken, the service passes to the other team. After this initial service, each team is permitted two handouts; i.e., each member of the team serves until his service is broken. After the second man of a team loses his serve, the service passes to the other team and the original order of service is followed thereafter. The team having the opening serve in the first game receives at the start of the second.

All the rules of long, short, and two-side serves, blocks and foot faults plus screen serves apply to each server. If a serve hits the man standing in the service box, the serve is replayed, but a fault serve hit before is not nullified.

A served ball passing behind the man in the service box is an automatic hinder and is replayed. If a man moves out of the service box before the served ball passes the short line, a fault is called. If he moves out of the box and is struck by the ball, handout is called.

Hinders are called in doubles, and both men of a doubles team must have a clear shot at the ball. If one partner swings at the ball and misses completely, his partner also has the right to an unobstructed shot. If his partner is hindered while attempting the shot, it is replayed.

Since four men are on the court, the chances are greater that players will be hit by the ball. If one player's shot hits his partner, the other team receives the serve or a point. If he hits one of the opposition with the ball before it touches the floor or front wall, the play is taken over with no penalty. If the ball rebounds from the front wall and hits an opponent, the other team receives a point or inflicts a handout, according to the situation.

The preceding are the basic rules of handball. Complete sets of rules can be found in libraries, sporting goods stores, or can be obtained by writing to the United States Handball Association or the Amateur Athletic Union (the addresses are in the bibliography).

SKILLS

Swing or Stroke, Hand Contact, and Positioning

The coordinated arm-wrist-hand swing, hand contact with the ball, and body position with respect to the ball—in conjunction with watching the ball—form the rudiments of handball.

The proper swing or stroke is a short, compact swing beginning from a "cocked" position, bent elbow (see Figs. 2-6a and 2-7a). The arm and hand are drawn back and as the ball is hit are pulled in fairly close to the body. The body faces a side wall at the beginning of the swing and rotates toward the front wall as the swing continues. The fingers are cupped only as much as is natural and are held together. The ball is struck with the part of the hand close to the base of the fingers. The ball can also be hit with the fist. However, this shot should not be attempted in the early stages of learning the game since the fist ball is so difficult to control.

A   B

C   D

FIGURE 2-6. Kill shot. (A) Beginning of proper kill shot stroke: arm cocked, elbow bent, body facing side wall. **(B)** Ball in glove, legs bent to lower body and hand close to floor, arm close to body. **(C)** Player continuing to watch ball as in A and B. **(D)** Kill shot completed; note follow through.

A

B

FIGURE 2-7. Offhand shot. (A) Start of offhand (left hand) stroke. Observe cocked arm position. (B) Continuation of offhand stroke; it is compact and travels through as short an arc as does the right hand in Fig. 2-6. Ball is in glove.

Figures 2-6 and 2-7 and the preceding paragraph convey only an approximation of good form. Every player hits the ball differently; the novice should not attempt to copy exactly the swing or form of another. Basically, the swing of the advanced player will be short, compact, and swift. It will be combined with body trunk rotation and proper body position with respect to the ball. His offhand swing will be almost a mirror image of his strong hand (see Fig. 2-7).

Characteristically, poor form includes a slow, ponderous, stiff swing, with the upper arm, forearm, and hand extended in line. That this form is inefficient is borne out by Holt (1969), who showed that the flexion-extension (flexed-elbow) stroke took less time and propelled the ball faster than the straight-arm stroke.

Beginners also suffer from another poor movement pattern—jumping or lunging at the ball. Since one cannot control his body movement when both feet are off the floor, one or preferably both feet should be on the floor during the execution of a shot. Being firmly planted on the floor is doubly important when returning hop shots. Since these shots change direction on the first bounce, they are almost impossible to return when a player is off balance or in the process of lunging at the ball.

The appropriate swing—underhand, sidearm, or overhand—depends on your position and the shot to be made. Even an over-the-shoulder or sidearm swing can be seen when a player has to run down a ball from behind. The ball is not caught or slung (which is illegal); it can be retrieved and hit from behind.

No matter how the ball is hit, some amount of follow through characterizes proper form. As you play, you will automatically follow through, as long as you are aware that you need to do this to avoid push shots or weak arm and hand movements. Do not try to steer the ball into the desired spot by pushing it. Swing fluidly. Pick the spot where you want to hit the ball, then concentrate on watching the ball. Even the veteran who forgets this rule usually does so with disastrous results.

It is difficult to program the swing, position, and hand contact into the brain simultaneously while watching the ball. But it is amazing how well it works, how soon you know your position in relation to the court and to the other player or players, and how accurately you can direct the ball when you watch the ball *before* and *during* the swing.

Once you have some idea of the proper swing, you must position yourself properly on the court in order to use it. Experience is the prime teacher here, but several rules of thumb may help. The first is to play the ball; do not let it play you. Watch the flight path and try to gauge the rebound so that you can position yourself to play the ball most easily. Do not run after the ball; let it come to you. When you see that the ball will bounce off a side wall, move to a spot behind the rebound point. Stay away from the point of rebound; otherwise the ball will bounce into you and severely restrict your swing. When the ball is angling across court, hit into the ball to drive it back to the front wall along roughly the same path (see Fig. 2-8).

There is another kind of position which complements your position on the court: the position of your body in relation to the flight of the ball at the time of the swing. Basically, each player picks some spot somewhere to the side and slightly forward and swings through this point of contact. To find this spot takes some experimenting; what may be comfortable for one player may not work for another. The exact point of contact also varies in relation to the shot to be made. Some shots are hit close to the floor; others may be hit high overhead. For example, positioning for shots off the back wall varies greatly among players. Some stoop over and let the ball drop almost to the

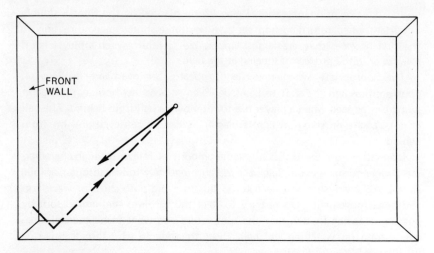

FIGURE 2-8. Dotted line represents front wall—side wall rebounding coming across court. Safest and easiest return is to drive the ball back along roughly the same angle; see arrow.

floor before hitting it. Others manage from an upright posture, but their percentage of kill shots is low.

Serving

Strong serves are a tremendous advantage to any handball player and may constitute about half a player's offensive strength. According to Pennington (1967), who designed and experimented with a series of special tests, a service placement test was the best measure of handball skill. Beginners who did well on this test, who could place their serves most accurately, were the best performers among their peers. Accuracy, the ability to hit the ball to the desired spot, is therefore important. This same accuracy, plus a repertoire of many serves and modifications of each, mark the skilled player.

The proper use of each serve demands thought. Do not serve the ball blindly. Remember the kind of serve hit last and especially the serve which gave the opposition the most trouble; then feed your opponent the same medicine with perhaps a slight change of speed and direction. Think about the serve before you hit the ball.

Before we describe the various serves, we want to warn you, as beginners, not to look back to watch the return of serve. You may get hit in the face with the ball. And receivers, do not hit short balls or other fault serves. It is poor etiquette and dangerous to the server, who may be turning around to catch a ball he thinks will be thrown gently to him.

If serving, move to center court immediately after the serve and get into position facing the front wall; the shot you must return will come from there. After you have played for some time, you can look back for clues as to where the receiver wants to hit the ball. Even then, simply glance back quickly and turn toward the front wall as the opponent begins his shot.

The lob serve (see Fig. 2-4) is usually learned first by the beginner because he wants to direct the ball into the back corners where some unexpected bounce will confuse his opponent. However, the lob serve is useful to all players since it requires the least energy expenditure of all the different serves.

This serve, which can be hit overhand (see Fig. 2-9) or underhand, brings the ball back in a high arc close to the ceiling. The ball can be lobbed to travel along the walls or across court.

The underhand lob is hit with a soft, bowling motion. The swing ends in a flick of the wrist to add a bit of overspin, which helps induce a high arc. If hit

FIGURE 2-9. Overhand serve can be hit hard or soft.

softly enough, the wall-hugging lob will bounce into a back corner and skid down along the back or side wall. The across-court version, if dropped against the side wall near the back wall, often kicks off the side wall and moves parallel to the back wall in a short bounce.

The next serve (see Figs. 2-3 and 2-10), called the power serve by some, is hit hard and low from a position facing a side wall and directed across court or along the walls into the rear corners. The ball is dropped gently and hit close to the floor with a swift wrist snap. It is driven just over the short line so fast and with such a flat bounce that the receiver has little time to return it.

The Z serve (angle or scotch toss, see Fig. 2-5) is hit very hard, underhand or overhand, across court from a position close to one side wall. The server may face a side wall or turn directly toward the front corner into which he wants to hit the ball. The ball rebounds from the front corner back across court with a spin which causes it to rebound off the side wall parallel to the back wall. If this serve comes into the side wall close enough to the back wall, it is very hard to handle. The other Z-serve variant, which bounces from the back to the side wall, can be equally tough.

These three basic serves—lob, power, and Z—must be mastered by the beginner, who should then experiment with variations of each.

The Three Basic Shots

The kill shot, the ceiling ball, and the pass shot are the three basic handball shots, although each has many variations.

FIGURE 2-10. Power serve hit hard and flat. Body and legs are bent to hit ball low.

The kill shot is the most spectacular. The ball strikes the front wall so low with so little rebound off the floor that it cannot be returned. This is the "money" ball, and some players develop such a fixation with the kill shot and attempt it so frequently that their over-all game deteriorates. No player should try to kill every shot. Depending on his position on the court and the position of the other player, it may be poor strategy to attempt a kill shot.

The front court is the ideal location from which to kill the ball, although an experienced player may attempt it from farther back depending on the position of his opponent. Most players take the ball as low as possible, whether on the fly or on the first bounce. The ball must be aimed as low as possible, either straight into the lowest spot (bottom board) on the front wall or into the front wall-side wall corners.

Shots off the back wall can also be made into kills. The back-wall shot is the delight of the advanced player and the bane of the beginner. Although the back-wall shot is theoretically one of the easiest to hit, since hand and ball are traveling in the same direction, it takes no small amount of skill to consistently perform well off the back wall. Like other kill shots, back-wall kills are directed into the corners or straight into the front wall. In addition to the speed which can be given this shot, it can also be made to hop by using wrist snap. As in other kill shots, most players let the rebound off the back wall drop close to the floor before they swing.

Position relative to the ball is also important. Beginners often move too close to the back wall and face it during execution of the shot. The proper positioning is shown in Fig. 2-11. Note how the player faces the side wall, concentrates on the ball, crouches to take the ball low, swings underhand, and moves forward slightly during the shot. He has positioned himself properly before the swing, not during it as many beginners do. He also swings underhand, avoiding the awkward sidearm or overhand stroke.

The next basic shot to be covered is the pass shot (see Fig. 2-12). This shot is the easiest, the most obvious, and the one most quickly learned. The ball is hit around or past the opposition by driving it along either side wall, against the wall next to a player, or into the greatest amount of open floor space.

Pass shots are hit from many court positions, including the back wall, and can be hit powerfully. The beginner should use the back-wall pass shot, mixing it with kill attempts from the same position rather than concentrating on the more spectacular kill shot. When the opposition holds the center court position, especially in doubles, the pass shot is often the better choice. A benefit of a hard hit, low pass shot is that the other man must chase it, which helps to tire and weaken him. Sometimes a fine pass-shot artist can control the game and wear down a man with superior kill abilities.

FIGURE 2-11. Back-wall shot. (A) Beginning of back-wall shot. As ball drops from back wall, player watches with arm positioned, waiting for ball to approach floor. (B) Ball has come out of glove on way to front wall. Note bent legs and slight crouch enabling player to release ball as low as possible. (C) Back-wall shot completed. Note follow through. Player has constantly watched ball.

The pass and kill shots are primarily offensive shots. The third, and final, basic shot, the ceiling ball, can be either offensive or defensive, depending on its execution. The two variations of the ceiling ball are the often-used overhand shot and the less-used underhand fist or bolo shot. The overhand shot should hit the ceiling some distance from the front wall so that the ball rebounds first off the front wall and then off the floor to carry over the player and drop down along the back wall to the floor. Hit well (see Fig. 2-13), the ceiling ball is difficult to handle on the first bounce or off the back wall and is therefore an offensive shot. It is defensive in that almost any ceiling ball that goes directly to the back wall forces the opposition to abandon the all-important center court position and move into back court. This statement leads into the cardinal rule of handball: the individual who gains

FIGURE 2-12. Sidearm shot about to be made; probably pass shot. Body is turned toward side wall, arm cocked.

FIGURE 2-13. Ceiling ball. (A) Player leans backward, eye on ball, elbow flexed in preparation. (B) Ball leaves glove, body bent slightly back to help direct ball upward. (C) Ball in flight to ceiling.

and holds the center court position will usually win, given two players roughly equal in skill.

The underhand or bolo shot, hit with the fist, may strike the ceiling first, in which case it behaves like an overhand ceiling ball. However, if it hits the front wall first, at the proper angle, it will rebound to graze the ceiling and drop to the floor. If it has enough spin and continues to the back wall, it may "bite" into the back wall, dropping sharply to the floor.

Fly Volleying

After his first few attempts to hit the ball in flight, the beginner often avoids fly volleys. He discovers that these shots hurt his hands much more than shots taken on the first bounce, and his errors and inaccuracy discourage him further. Nevertheless, fly volleying is necessary to maintain the important center court position and must be learned.

The prime difficulty is to gauge correctly the flight of the ball, and experience is the only teacher. The player should position himself so that the ball passes him, preferably on his strong-hand side. If he must move out of center court, he should move back in immediately after the shot to be ready for subsequent shots. If he can stay in center court, the other man will have to chase the ball and will operate at a disadvantage from back court.

Fly volleying, however, is more than simply staying in center court and hitting the ball. Each shot should be made with something special in mind. For example, if the opponent is on one side, hit the ball hard and low down the other side. The ball can also be driven high into the front corners to bring it across court so that it bounces in the back corners. An especially good shot for a right-handed player is to bring the ball across court into the left back corner.

Fly Kill

The most devastating shot in handball is the fly kill. It is also the most difficult to learn. Hit in flight as it rebounds off the front wall (another approach is to take the ball off a side wall), the ball is aimed into the front corners or into the bottom board of the front wall.

The problem is to gauge the path of the rebound of the previous shot. The player must predict where the ball will contact the floor and position himself so that the ball drops close to him, preferably on his strong-hand side. No matter how nerve-wracking it may be, he must wait until the ball is close to the floor before hitting it with a sidearm swing.

The fly kill is usually attempted from somewhere near the service or short lines. Position is all important; the player must be under the descending ball and should be stationary at the time of the swing. To keep the point of contact low, many players crouch or stoop. If the player is right handed and is attempting a right-hand shot, he should face the right wall. When executing a left-hand kill, turn the body toward the left side wall. Avoid facing the front wall. Do not try underhand or bolo-type fly kills; they are more risky and inaccurate than sidearm shots. Aim some fly kills into the corners, others into the front wall to keep the opposition off balance.

FIST AND TRAP SHOTS

Once a player has attained some all-around handball ability, he can attempt the fist and trap shots. Hitting the ball with the fist imparts more speed to the ball in volleying and helps to put added zip into ceiling balls and around-the-wall shots made with the weak hand. Made with a full overhand swing, the around-the-wall fist shot rebounds from side to front to side wall very swiftly. Moving across court in its flight toward the back wall, the ball is as difficult to hit accurately in flight from the center court position as it is from back court, where it often takes unexpected bounces because of speed and angle of rebound.

The overhand fist stroke can also be used to add extra speed to pass shots or ceiling balls. More common, however, is a "punch" ball. More players favor this kind of fist shot—hit with a very short swing, either partial sidearm or underhand bolo style—because it is inherently more accurate than a full swing and imparts almost as much speed. Generally, the punch shot is executed with the weak hand, although there are exceptions.

All these shots are useful when the ball must be hit hastily or from a poor position. Sometimes a man simply cannot swing strongly, and the fist or punch is the only way to generate sufficient speed.

In addition to extra speed, fist balls have the added virtue of often behaving differently from open-hand shots in terms of angle of rebound and subsequent path toward the back wall. It is extremely disconcerting for an opponent to set up under what appears to be an easy fly kill only to find that he has misjudged the flight path of the ball.

The trap shot is made similar to the way an infielder makes a one-hand stab at a hot grounder or a line drive bouncing at his feet. Instead of catching the ball, however, it is struck on the first bounce with an underhand bowling motion and aimed low at the front wall or a front corner. Another version of the kill, the trap shot is an excellent way to handle shots which bounce close to and in front of the player and can be hit so quickly that the opposition can rarely return a well-executed shot.

SPIN AND HOP

After one game with a player who hits the ball with spin, the novice is acutely aware that he must acquire this skill if he wants to be a successful handball player. A ball hit with spin, hops (see Fig. 2-3) or changes direction when it hits the floor. Adding a new dimension to the game, hop comes from spin put on the ball by whipping the hand across some part of the ball, rather than hitting straight through it. The motion of the hand sliding across the ball is aided by forearm-wrist swivel.

Many players have some natural forearm-wrist swivel which must be amplified to generate enough spin to make the ball hop. Right-handed players, for example, can apply spin which makes the ball hop left on hard serves hit straight back toward the rear corners. The forearm and wrist must be swiveled to whip the hand across the bottom left part of the ball as it rebounds from the floor.

To make the ball hop right is not as easily achieved by the right hander. The ball must be hit by whipping the hand over the right side of the ball, a more awkward motion than that causing the ball to hop to the left. However, the technique can be mastered. Left handers using the same strokes previously described will generate hop just the reverse of that obtained by right handers.

It takes some time to learn the stroke, and it is not always easy to remember just what you have done after you hit a good hop ball, which can make it difficult to duplicate the same movement. In any event, hop serves can be tremendously effective, especially when the server can apply right or left hop at will. The receiver can then be made to lunge for a ball moving away from him or can be handcuffed by a ball bouncing into him.

Shots other than the serve can also be made more effective with hop. One is the back-wall shot, perhaps the easiest shot to make hop. The natural underhand forearm-wrist movement with which this shot is hit puts a great deal of spin on the ball which can be increased with little effort. Kill shots can also be improved with hop. A well-placed, hard-hit kill is doubly difficult to return if it changes direction on the first bounce.

ANTICIPATION

Anticipation is the ability to move with minimum effort to the location which best allows the return of the opponent's shot. To do this, the player reads his opponent's moves to predict the shot he will make and the resulting flight path of the ball. For example, see Fig. 2-14: the player in back court is hurrying forward, having anticipated the forthcoming kill shot.

Anticipation is the key to handball. It is the mark of the improving player. Being able to foresee the next shot allows economy of movement; it is the essence of being in the right place at the right time. The novice often wonders why a more experienced player always seems to be at the right place on the court. Since the game requires swift movement and equally swift decisions, the beginner soon realizes that his opponent knows where the ball is going at about the same time he prepares to hit it.

There is no magic involved in this ability to so accurately forecast the next shot. Predictions are based on visual cues—some obvious, some subtle—of body and head position and of arm movements. For example, if a man is bending over to take the ball as low as possible, the experienced player moves quickly alongside or almost in front of him. When a player stoops over waiting for the ball to drop low, a kill shot is coming, and it is no time to linger in the back court. Likewise, if the other man quickly positions himself under a poorly hit return, facing the side wall or a front corner, the wise player will move up quickly, knowing a fly kill is probable. On pass shots,

FIGURE 2-14. Back court player hurries forward knowing from opponent's body position that kill attempt is likely.

many players shift their shoulders or their entire body distinctively, forecasting the side to which they will hit the ball. As soon as these visual cues register, move into the side of the court where you expect the ball to be hit. You will then be poised to return it swiftly and accurately.

When you see the opposing player leaning backward with a high bounce coming to him, a ceiling ball is in the offing. As soon as he begins the overhand swing characteristic of the ceiling ball stroke, drift back toward the back wall if you intend to take the shot there or move into the front court area quickly if that is your choice. The point is not to get caught in midcourt under the highest part of the bounce or to be in the process of running backward or forward. Both mistakes make a return of this hard-to-handle shot doubly difficult. Again, you must position yourself to return the ball from a steady stance.

Anticipation is also important when returning a Z serve or a volley shot hit sharply into a front wall corner. Such a shot comes off the side wall almost perpendicular to the side wall. Unless the rebound is anticipated and the player positions himself away from the wall and only slightly in back of the spot at which the ball contacts the wall (see Fig. 2-15), he will be able to do little more than wave at the ball. Many players never seem to recognize this shot and are constantly confused by it.

Watch the server closely. If he seems to serve without noting your position, edge forward to intercept the rebound on the fly and smash it down along the wall or around the server. This sudden bit of unexpected violence can do much to unnerve the server. If he has a good lob serve that you cannot return well from the back corner, run forward and hit the ball on the fly. In each case, the server gives away his intentions by his actions. If the server puts an exceeding amount of hop on the ball, try to move laterally slightly to be in the best position, or move up and take the ball close to its point of contact with the floor to minimize the effect of hop.

There are many other such instances where anticipation is important. Anticipation and proper subsequent play comes only through experience. Watch the better men play. Observe how they watch their opponents and move unerringly to the path of the rebound. There are very few shots that cannot be returned if you anticipate correctly. Anticipating quickly and correctly early in the game is good strategy, as it is most unsettling to many players to watch their best shots turned into kills or impossible-to-return pass shots.

Anticipation is as important in doubles as it is in singles. For example, a man may be trapped behind an opponent who is trying to kill the ball in the corner directly in front of him. His partner must then forsake his normal position and move across and into the front court to play the probable kill.

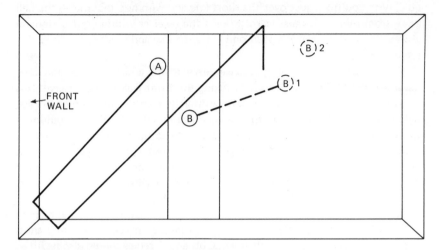

FIGURE 2-15. Player A hits ball across court into left front corner, and ball moves across court to right side wall. Player B should move to position 1 and not to position 2 to best return ball rebounding off side wall parallel to back wall.

He must sense the position and predicament of his partner as well as those of the other team. Doubles play seems to ebb and flow about the court, and each man must be ready to move out of his zone to support his partner. Anticipation helps him do this.

SERVICE TACTICS

The beginner who wishes to upgrade his serves can best do this by learning a variety of serves and using each with varying speeds and angles, by serving different serves from same court position, by quickly analyzing opponent's weaknesses in terms of service returns, and by developing both kinds of hop serves. All these suggestions emphasize one fact underscoring good serving—be unpredictable in your choice of serves and vary speed and angle when you do hit two of the same kind in succession.

Concentrate on each serve and try to accomplish something with each. Too many handball players, some of them advanced, simply hit the serve with little thought of doing anything other than putting the ball in play. The serve should be your best offensive weapon. For example, if your opponent prefers to await your serve standing in the left side of the court, drill a low, hard serve into the right corner. This serve causes him to move laterally very quickly if you hit it just over the short line and with hop that moves the ball away from him. You must learn to keep the receiver within your peripheral vision. Know the receiver's position before serving, and practice the hard, flat serve.

One reason so many players never learn to hit a hard serve is that they never escape the beginner's trait of facing the front wall during a serve. It is almost impossible to hit the ball with authority from this position or to keep it low, since the hand moves through an upward path. The player should face the side wall, lining up as though he was going to hit a golf ball through the front wall. To try a hard serve, drop the ball gently, crouch down to hit it very low off the floor and whip the hand through the ball in a shallow, flat arc, aiming it just over the short line. Experiment with different wrist movements until you can hit the ball hard and flat with hop.

Keep these hard serves low. Do not hit them so that they rebound high on the back wall. Any experienced player can take such back-wall set-up shots and do whatever he wants with them. Lob and Z serves should also be hit so that they bounce in the rear corners at angles to the back wall which make them difficult to return.

To practice lob shots, you should try to lob the ball on a very high arc so that it descends into one of the rear corners and contacts the side wall first. Often the ball will not carry to the back wall or will travel in a short bounce parallel to the back wall. If your opponent seems sluggish or is inclined to wait for back-wall shots, hit a high lob serve which carries just over the short line and bounces high to fall into the rear corner.

In addition to practicing soft lob shots, try to master the Z serve. Hit the ball into the front wall-side wall corner as hard as you can. Experiment until the resulting rebound off the side wall comes straight out close to and paralleling the back wall. Seldom can this serve be returned strongly.

After you have learned to hit the lob, power, and Z (or scotch toss) serves, try varying the speed and angle of each from time to time. Serve from different positions between the short and service lines and move immediately into the center court position to await the return.

Try not to telegraph your intentions. Learn to hit serves to different locations from the same serving position. For example, if you have served into the left rear corner from the left side several times and your opponent is beginning to edge over to the left side in anticipation of a similar serve, hit a low, hard serve into the right rear corner or a Z serve into the left rear corner from the same stance. Keep the majority of your serves moving to your opponent's weak hand. Serve only occasionally to his strong hand to keep him honest.

If you try for a crotch serve (a ball rolling dead on the floor out of the side wall-floor seam), aim at a point along the side wall farthest from the receiver. If he is loafing in left rear court, shoot a low flat serve just over the short line in the right side-wall crotch.

The least that can be expected of the serve is a weak return; the best is an ace. Work hard on the serve; it is your best offensive weapon.

CAUTIONS AND SAFETY PRINCIPLES

Handball players do not need to undergo extreme muscular strain or to indulge in body contact, and these two factors make handball the low-risk sport that it is. To further reduce the possibility of injury, players should observe the following safety factors.

Never look directly at the man hitting the ball. If you must watch the hitter, glance out of the corner of your eyes. Better yet, raise your hand or arm and peek out from under it. If you wear safety glasses or the wire or plastic eye guards and follow the preceding rule, the chances of eye injury are almost nil.

Respect for the rules of the game, especially the hinder, will also help avoid injury. For example, if the other man blocks your path to the ball, do not run into him. Simply call a hinder. If you are close to him and the ball passes between you, do not swing at it. This not only prevents injury to him; but you may also well avoid a badly wrenched arm.

When a ball is skidding along the wall and you have to hit it, place your hand next to the wall and slide it along the wall into the ball. This prevents the pain of sore knuckles or bruised fingers resulting from a swing made in an arc that takes the hand into the wall.

The hand is not the only part of the body to be kept away from the walls. Beginners are cautioned especially to know where they are on the court and not to crash into walls in a headlong charge. For all players, we want to stress that you move immediately out of the back court to avoid a collision with the opponent who is trying to retrieve a ceiling ball or some other shot carrying to this location. Since he will turn and come back after the ball (at the beginning of his turn he cannot see you) and you can see him, it is your responsibility to get out of his way.

When people move at the pace they do in handball, they sweat. And sweat or any moisture on the floor makes footing treacherous. To avoid a bad fall, wipe up sweat spots; if someone does fall, dry the floor where he fell.

The last point to be made concerns care of the hands. Sore hands, particularly deep, painful bone bruises, seem to afflict almost every handballer at some point in his career. Soaking the hands in hot water prior to a game is one way of preventing soreness and bruises. The slight swelling induced by the hot water seems to cushion the bones. When bone bruises do occur, players have two choices. They can discontinue play until the injury heals or try to play with padded gloves or padding taped over the sensitive spot. A thorough warm-up also reduces the chances of sore hands as well as of other injuries. Refer to Chapter 5 for warm-up procedures.

BEFORE PROCEEDING FURTHER, YOU SHOULD UNDERSTAND:

The basic rules of the game.

The three basic serves (lob, power, and Z), the three basic shots (kill, ceiling, and pass), and the importance and technique of each.

The principles of swing, hand contact, positioning, hop, and anticipation.

The usefulness of fly volleying and of the fly kill, fist and trap shots.

The basic safety precautions every player should take when playing handball.

II

One Step
Further

3

HANDBALL
its history and place
in american life today

This chapter will explain:
The origin of handball and how it has come
to be accepted by America

About 1882, an Irishman named Phil Casey left his native land and settled in Brooklyn. Casey might have been just another immigrant except for the fact that he was a master handball player. That Casey excelled at handball was not surprising. The game originated in Ireland in the 11th or 12th century and had grown into an Irish national sport by the 1800s. The game, then known as "fives" (because of the use of the five fingers), was also played by the British.

Casey was not entirely satisfied with the New World. He could find no handball players except other expatriates, and when he did, there were no courts on which he could adequately display his talents. His solution was to obtain financing and build a 65' long, 25' wide handball court with a 30' high front wall and 25' high side walls. Those who played, paid, and it is said that with the revenue from this court Casey built others.

In 1887, Casey and the Irish handball champion, John Lawlor, met in an international match to decide the world handball championship. Twenty-one games were to be played if necessary; the first man to win 11 games was to be declared the champion. The first 10 were to be played in Cork, Ireland; the remainder in Casey's Brooklyn court. The two contenders bet $1000 on the outcome.

Lawlor won six of the 10 games played in Cork on an 80' by 40' court. Once back in the United States, however, Casey came on strong to win seven straight games to take the championship. He retired undefeated in 1900.

Another early handball stalwart was Michael Eagan from Galway, Ireland. He learned to play on his brother's court in Jersey City and developed so swiftly that he was able to win the first hard ball handball tournament held under the auspices of the Amateur Athletic Union in 1897. Eagan was a hard hitter in contrast to Casey, who had a more deliberate style emphasizing placement of the ball.

In the following years, handball found favor in America. Frank Menke (1969) says, "There wasn't a fireman in the land who didn't devote some of his leisure to playing handball against the side of the firehouse." Along the New York and Jersey coasts, the one-wall brand developed as bathers banged tennis balls off the sides of bath houses. By 1910, one-wall courts were constructed at the Brighton and Manhattan beaches, which helps to explain the popularity of the one-wall game on the east coast.

A few years later, the Detroit Athletic Club gave the sport a boost by building several fine four-wall courts and in 1915 held an invitational tournament, won by Fritz Seivered of Cleveland. The game gained slowly in popularity over the years until the United States Handball Association (USHA) was formed in 1950. Under the impetus of the USHA's strong promotional campaigns, growth has been such that today an estimated 4.5 million aficionados hit the ball around the walls at YMCA, athletic club, and university courts.

The game has changed much since Casey's time. A softer, livelier ball is in play, and the courts have shrunk—40' X 20' X 20' courts are now standard, although odd sizes exist.

Even more astonishing to Casey would be the new glass-walled courts which make four-wall handball a spectator sport. The rules have also changed. In his era, players could and would kick the ball, a technique still practiced in the Irish game.

On the American scene, doctors, lawyers, salesmen, engineers, college professors—people of all ranks and vocations—flock to the courts. Women too have begun to play, as have more teenagers every year. More tournaments, including some in the collegiate and junior brackets, are being held every year. National sports magazines now cover the national championships, and a new complex of courts designed especially for television coverage is being built. Handball has been taken out of the sweaty, dingy courts where it remained for so long and thrust into the limelight with the advent of the glass-walled courts. As more leisure time becomes available and more people recognize the value of conditioning, handball will be an even larger part of the American sports scene.

YOU SHOULD NOW KNOW THAT:

The Irish played handball some 700 years before bringing the game to America in the late 1800s.

More than 4.5 million people play handball in the United States.

Through the strong promotional efforts of the United States Handball Association, handball is increasing in popularity every day.

4

PHYSIOLOGICAL, PSYCHOLOGICAL, AND SOCIOLOGICAL BENEFITS

This chapter will tell you:
What handball has to offer you as a player

Handball is a high-energy-expenditure activity; it is therefore an efficient method of exercising. Only 60 to 90 minutes of handball three times a week will trim off fat (if proper eating habits are maintained) and improve cardio-respiratory endurance. For the average person, the sport provides a year-round way to attain a high level of physical fitness, and the well-conditioned athlete can retain his fitness through regular play.

The strenuous nature of handball, recognized by all players, has been borne out by research. Banister and co-workers (1964) substantiated this fact, as did a study by Tumbull (1964), which revealed that 10 weeks of handball significantly improved the cardio-respiratory fitness of men of college age.

An efficient physical fitness program, coupled with excitement and competition, is always in demand. This demand basically explains the growth of handball, for the game is neither boring nor repetitious, and it is competitive. The many bounces the ball can take, the many angles of rebound, the ways in which a player can vary his strategy, all introduce infinite variety into each game.

Yet another factor is the ease with which an individual can select the intensity of exercise he desires. If he wants the heaviest workout, he may play singles. To decrease the amount of exercise, he may choose the cutthroat game. The least amount of exercise comes from doubles. Few sports allow the intensity of exercise to be changed so easily.

Handball also offers little risk of injury when compared with many other sports. In a competitive game involving people of varying ages, it is important that they be able to play without constant fear of injury. Of course, handball players do occasionally suffer a sore arm, a bruised hand, or minor aches and pains, but rarely do they break bones, dislocate shoulders, or experience serious muscle pulls. Handball is much more a game of wits, swift movement, coordination, and experience than a test of brute strength.

This combination of low risk and the edge given by experience is what makes handball so useful as a conditioner for so many people. On the local courts, many men in their 30s and 40s and some even older can outthink and therefore outplay younger, quicker, and stronger men. In doubles, two such cagey veterans who have played together for some time operate like well-oiled machinery to defeat younger teams. Unlike champion swimmers who reach their peak in their teens, handball champions hit their stride around the age of 30.

To keep people interested over a long period of time, a sport must offer more than physical conditioning. Almost every handball player points to the fact that he can totally lose himself in the game. It is this total absorption of mind and body which is so attractive—people today look for activities to help them forget their problems and to recharge their spiritual batteries.

The mental benefits of handball stem from the intense concentration required by all facets of the game, from the complexities of court strategy to the basics of watching and hitting the ball. The art of quickly finding an opponent's weakness demands undivided attention. These and all the other factors of play woven into a rapidly changing situation demand complete concentration. Nor can this concentration falter. Handball begins and continues at top speed. Few time outs, delays, or equipment changes occur; the rules limit them. There are no actionless periods as there are in some other sports. There is no time for reflection other than on the game, which makes handball as useful for mental diversion or release of tension as it is for physical conditioning.

Although handball is a gentleman's game requiring considerable personal integrity and ethics, keen competition pervades it. The rankest beginner recognizes the joy of running his opponent back and forth across the court until he is unable to catch up with the ball. Satisfaction comes from maneuvering your opponent into the back court and then smashing the ball into the bottom board, from which it rolls out on the floor. Just as satisfying are hard-hit pass shots or delicately stroked ceiling balls. Whatever the shot, you pit yourself against the other man, running him, forcing him into a bad shot, or simply not giving him an opportunity to return the ball. Ample competition always exists; in any group of handballers there is always someone better or just as good as you are.

Handball also has some sociological benefits. After acquiring some expertise, the newcomer can find a circle of handball friends to fit into. Indeed, he will progress faster if he seeks out the better players. As he becomes more proficient his presence will become an advantage to this group. In this way, the game is a social asset, as are other sports and accomplishments. In fact, some say handballers already constitute a "players fraternity."

IN SUMMARY:

As a game requiring a high level of expenditure of energy, handball provides both exercise and conditioning.

The possibility of any injury is slight, while the probability of serious injury is remote.

Handball provides a social recreational activity of varying physical intensity for people of all ages.

5

APPLICATION OF THE PRINCIPLES OF MOTOR LEARNING

This chapter will cover:
1. A few principles of motor learning
2. How to condition yourself for handball
3. How to practice

Although overpowering muscular strength is not required in handball, the necessary development of the offhand and the surprisingly large speed and agility requirements lead some people to discontinue play because of disappointingly poor performance in the first few games. To prepare these people for such problems and to help them develop appropriate skills, some motor learning principles are helpful.

1. The individual must be motivated adequately for motor learning to occur, whether the motivation comes from within himself or from some outside source (Singer, 1968).

2. Improvement in certain phases may be inhibited by poor general physical fitness or by some specific fitness component (Singer, 1968).

3. Repeating movement patterns is essential to the development of skills. However, practicing, and consequently ingraining, incorrect movements delays the development of proper motions. This fact accents the need for adequate instruction during early stages of motor learning (Singer, 1968).

4. Since handball demands speed *and* accuracy, both should be developed simultaneously. For example, constantly hitting the ball with a slow, easy swing can lead to movement patterns which will have to be altered when the beginner wishes to accentuate speed (Johnson, 1966).

5. Many short practice sessions are better than a few long ones, since the fatigue incurred in a long practice session can incorrectly influence movement patterns (Seyffarth, 1940).

During the first few games, the beginner often leaves the court with a feeling of frustration caused by his inability to cope with the fast-moving ball and the seeming impossibility of interpreting the angle of rebound from the walls or ceiling and the direction of bounce off the floor. Generally, the beginner responds too quickly and wastes a great deal of motion and energy. His skill develops as he learns to sort visual cues quickly and as he needs less visual information to produce the necessary stimulus for proper movement. Although this process of development seems so difficult, the novice can take comfort from the fact that the most sophisticated computer and robot systems of today do not have nearly enough intelligence or mobility to play handball.

CONDITIONING AND PRACTICE

Handballers, in contrast to players of other sports, need very little off-the-court conditioning or practice (in terms of serving, volleying, fly killing by themselves). The game itself is almost all the practice and conditioning one needs.

Our only recommendation to the beginner for conditioning is that he do some running to develop over-all stamina and cardio-respiratory endurance (wind). The beginner needs plenty of "wind" plus some over-all strength, including a sound pair of legs. But after roughly three to six months of steady playing (maybe less if in good condition), he will develop an adequate level of fitness. The authors, who have been playing for several years, doubt that a program of running, unless a very strenuous one, in conjunction with regular play would contribute much to the endurance required for handball.

In the past other authorities have recommended weight exercises to strengthen the wrists and forearms. Again, a reasonable amount of wrist and forearm strength is necessary, yet handball requires a swift arm movement, which really does not lend itself to improvement by weight exercises. In fact, many handball players with average or even thin arms hammer the ball fiercely by virtue of a quick, whipping motion. Indeed, this whip movement suggests flexibility, something the handballer should strive for. Before practice or play, light calisthenics are suggested, and this is about the extent of the conditioning most players accept. Sit-ups and push-ups are in this category of conditioning. Run in place, touch your toes, twist your body. In general, be sure you are completely loosened up before practice or play.

In addition to whatever conditioning value these exercises have, they are valuable in preventing muscle pulls, pinched nerves, and sore arms. Hand conditioning is also important for the seasoned player as well as for the beginner. The beginner should wear padded gloves and both he and the advanced player should build up the tempo of pre-game or pre-practice activity from throwing and catching the ball, to throwing and striking it lightly, to throwing and hitting it as hard as he would in a game. In addition, all players might well soak their hands in hot water prior to the game for the reasons set forth in the section on cautions and safety principles.

For those who wish to practice, the same conditioning and warm-up exercises are recommended. Handball practice is relatively easy, since the ball cannot escape or travel as far as it can in tennis, golf, or some other sports.

Serving practice should be most productive for the beginner. Experimentation is the word. Serve often, attempt all the serves, and try to accurately place them. Try to direct the same serve, the lob serve, for example, to the same spot with variations of speed and flight path. Try a lob serve into the left back-wall corner and then blast a power serve to the same location. Such practice improves accuracy.

Attempt the kill shots. Throw the ball so it comes off the side wall close to the serving zone and try to kill the rebound. Throw the ball straight into the front wall and try for front-wall and front-corner kills, hitting the ball as close to the floor as possible. Try fly killing, throwing the ball to the front wall and waiting for the rebound to come close to the floor. In this shot, position is important, so lob the ball to the front wall and move under the rebound.

Practice back-wall shots, especially kills. Let the ball come as low as possible. Try to shoot the ball around the walls from back wall and fire it up against the ceiling. Lob ball against front wall and practice ceiling balls. Work to drop ceiling balls into back corners.

Do not neglect practice with the offhand. Throw the ball with your weak hand and hit all the shots with it. Try kills, hard pass shots, around-the-walls, ceiling balls—all the shots. Nothing will improve your game more than offhand practice and the subsequently greater dexterity.

Pre-game warm up and practice consists of the same procedures already set forth. Make sure you are "loose," your hands are warmed up, and that you have practiced the various shots to regain timing and body positioning. Do not let anyone hurry your warm up. A couple of minutes extra playing time is not worth a bone bruise, a pinched nerve, or a pulled muscle.

FROM THIS CHAPTER, YOU SHOULD HAVE LEARNED THAT:

You must be properly motivated to learn and should practice in short rather than in long sessions.

Other than actually playing, very few practice or conditioning exercises are necessary.

You must warm up slowly and thoroughly before a game.

6

MECHANICAL PRINCIPLES

In this chapter, you will be introduced to:
Those mechanical principles that influence performance

Handball is a relatively simple game played without implements, such as racquets or paddles, in a small court. Nevertheless there are a few mechanical factors which influence performance. They do so in three basic areas: (1) motions of the players themselves, (2) contacting the ball, and (3) interplay of the ball with the walls, ceiling, and floor.

An obvious, though seldom mentioned fact, is that the most successful handball players are men of average size. As mentioned before, extreme height is not necessary: high shots can be played as they bounce off the back wall, but shots near the floor level are more quickly and easily reached by the shorter player. The lively ball and relatively small playing area create a very high volleying rate. From a mechanics standpoint, the person with longer, heavier limbs has more difficulty performing the necessary movements at the required speed than does the smaller man. These are important factors in the development of champions. However, these facts do not mean that tall, heavy people cannot play and enjoy the game; nor does it mean that the smaller man will automatically walk away with the trophies.

In executing most shots, the physical law of inertia plays a large part. The beginner's stiff-armed roundhouse-type motion, especially in shoulder-high shots, robs him of hand velocity that adds speed to the ball. Because the arm is straight rather than bent at the elbow, there is more inertia, or greater resistance to motion, and less hand velocity in the beginner's movement. The desired motion is similar to the baseball pitcher's movements, made with a flexed elbow and cocked wrist, as the upper arm rotates forward. As the point of release is approached, the elbow extends followed by flexion of the wrist. This same principle applies in handball. This limb motion generates the highest hand velocity possible, a fact demonstrated experimentally by Holt in 1969.

The principle of correct limb movement applies also to the rest of the body. Stepping into the ball from a position facing the side wall and rotating the trunk forward is an essential motion preceding forward arm movement. Again, the step is made to position the body before the shot—the player should work to position himself so that every shot, including the actual arm movement, is made from a stationary position.

Failure to bring one or more body segments into motion at the proper time forces an awkward, inefficient shot. Some players do not demonstrate a mechanically efficient style, although they seem fairly successful. However, they will never reach their full potential until they learn proper body movements.

Correct body movements are extremely important in handball's premier play, the kill shot. Beginners are often unable to develop this shot because they do not position the body properly. They tend to face the front wall, which forces them to return many shots with an upward, bowling-like swing (with fingers pointing toward floor at contact). It is therefore difficult to hit the ball accurately, especially low on the front wall. If only a small directional error occurs as the ball rolls out of the hand, the ball will hit the floor or strike too high on the front wall. However, if the hand is swung in a plane parallel to the floor as it should be, the same error will do little harm to the accuracy of the shot. The ball will merely strike a bit to the right or left of the intended spot on the wall.

Mechanical principles are also involved in ball-hand contact and the problem of propelling the ball with all possible speed. Speed results from "catching" the ball and accelerating it while it is in contact with the hand. Since acceleration is a function of force and the length of time that force is applied, it follows that "catching and throwing" the ball with maximum wrist motion provides the greatest amount of time (and contact) and therefore the greatest speed.

The low speed a newcomer applies to the ball is evident. One reason for this lack of speed is that he uses an open hand and a stiff wrist. The result is that the hand is in contact with the ball for a very brief time when compared to the advanced player's wrist whip or snap. Hence the beginner's ball propulsion speed is proportionately less.

Shots off the back wall furnish the best opportunity for high-speed shots. In this case, the ball is already traveling toward the front wall; it does not have to be stopped and restarted again as would a ball off the front or side wall. Hand speed must be high, though, to catch up to the ball and boost it on its way.

The fist shot varies from the open-hand shot in that the heel of the hand, the fingers, or the knuckles provides a rigid surface with which to hit the ball. In the open-hand shot the hand and wrist action absorbs the energy of the ball in stopping it and sending it in the opposite direction. In the fist shot, the energy of the ball is not completely absorbed at contact; it is stored in the ball as it compresses against the hand. This energy is regained—the ball expands—as it "flys" off the fist. This expansion adds to ball velocity and gives resultant high speed even though the contact time is short.

The third area of handball affected by mechanical principles concerns hop and the fundamentals of angle of contact and rebound. It should be noted here that hop is very hard to achieve on a fist shot because of the short time the hand is in contact with the ball.

The bounces and the resulting rapid changes in direction, angle, and speed of the ball drive the beginner to the point where some quit after only a game or two. It seems impossible to follow the ball or to move into position to hit it. However, most shots follow the well-known principle: the angle of contact equals the angle of rebound (similar to the case of light, where the angle of incidence equals the angle of reflection). After contact between the ball and walls, ceiling, and floor, the ball, therefore, generally moves along a predictable path, and experience soon teaches a player how to anticipate which way the ball will go. Correct positioning then follows. But, should spin be put on the ball so that it hops and varies from the normal or predicted direction, a new element of uncertainty is introduced.

Our discussion of spin and hop is divided into two parts: bounces off the front and side wall and contact with the floor. Front- and side-wall variations are outlined first.

The natural wrist and hand action of a right-handed player spins the ball clockwise around an axis perpendicular to the floor. If a shot is hit directly to the front wall, the rebound deviates from the expected path. That is, if the ball is hit from the right side of the court to the middle of the front wall, the ball rebounds at an angle less than the contact angle and follows a path to the left of that expected. A shot hit by a right hander from the left side of the court "bites" into the wall and rebounds at a greater angle than expected. The ball tends to lose its spin during contact and move directly toward the back wall. In either case, the rebound moves along a path left of that expected. The reverse is the case with a left-hand shot: counterclockwise spin is generated and the ball moves to the right of the anticipated path. If the ball is hit head on into the front wall, little or no variation in rebound angle is observed.

Another example of this kind of spin occurs in the side wall-front wall kill shot. If a right hander hits a low shot to the right side wall (with clockwise spin), the ball rebounds at a lesser angle than that of contact with little loss of spin and carries to the front wall near the corner. If he hits the same shot against the left wall, the ball bites into the wall, coming off at a greater angle than that of contact and probably not reaching the front wall. The side wall-front wall kill shot from the left therefore must strike the side closer to the front wall than the same shot from the right side of the court.

Overspin and underspin (backspin) also vary the rebounds from the front wall. Overspin can be and often is used in the lob serve to cause the ball to rise from the front wall (lesser angle of rebound) and travel to the back court in a higher arc than normal. Underspin applied to ceiling balls and pass shots results in rebounds at lesser angles and the ball reaches the floor sooner than it would if no spin were applied.

In the preceding paragraphs, the effects of sidespin, overspin and underspin have been explained. In these spins, the ball rotates closely about an axis perpendicular or parallel to the floor. The effect of spin in which the ball rotates about axes tilted away from these two axes is less easily understood. Although many authorities have expressed their opinions concerning the techniques and action of these shots, there is little evidence to explain precisely how the ball acts.

The following explanation represents the opinion of the authors based on their experience, observation, and study of the mechanics involved. Either clockwise or counterclockwise spin (looking from the back of the ball as it moves toward the front wall) can be applied by cutting across the ball at contact. It is easier and more natural for a right hander to apply clockwise motion; for a left hander, counterclockwise. Both spins, however, can be developed with practice.

The authors believe that the direction of the spin of the ball is reversed when the ball is driven straight against the front wall. A ball spinning clockwise rebounds with the reverse spin and hops to the left when it touches the floor. A shot moving toward the front wall and spinning counterclockwise will rebound and hop to the right.

YOU SHOULD, AFTER READING
THIS CHAPTER, UNDERSTAND WHY:

A flexed elbow and a cocked wrist, in conjunction with proper body movements, give maximum ball velocity.

A swing made parallel to the floor is inherently more accurate than a bowling-like swing.

The direction of hop depends on the direction of spin and the angle of contact.

7

STRATEGY

This chapter is a brief introduction to:
The kinds of tactics employed for successful
singles and doubles play

THE SINGLES GAME

Singles strategy is very simple—keep your opponent running; hit the ball away from him. If you can do this, your opponent will be able to do little more than retrieve the ball and play defensive handball, which is what you want to accomplish. Since he is moving, he will not be able to set or position himself for the best execution of any shot and very likely will furnish you with the opportunity to kill the ball or make some other shot to end the volley. Many players never seem to learn to keep the ball away from their opponent. Rather, they concentrate on a few pet shots which their opponent soon learns to expect. Once your opponent can key in on these shots (predict your performance), your control of the game is lost. Base your strategy, therefore, on the court position of your opposition and that of yourself and not merely on execution of a few shots.

Because strategy fluctuates with changing court position, it is impossible to form hard and fast rules. However, two general ones should be kept in mind: (1) move into center court immediately after serving and attempt to hold this position during the volley and (2) when in front of your opponent, try to kill the ball; when in back of him, hit pass shots.

The game of handball can be controlled from the center court position. At center court, the ball can best be cut off and fly killed or fly volleyed. Here, less energy needs to be expended in volleying and controlling the game. In addition, any imperfectly executed kill or pass shot attempted from in back of you can be recovered and turned into a kill.

If possible, as soon as you hit a shot from the back court, move into the center court. To cause the opposing player to vacate center court, hit ceiling balls, hard pass shots, or an around-the-walls shot. After you have forced him back, do not stand around in back court waiting for his return. Move immediately into center court; hold this position by fly volleying or try to end the volley with a fly kill. Remember, you cannot play the game successfully from back court.

Rule two, that of killing the ball when in front of the opposition and passing when in back, stems from some basic facts of court positioning. When you are in front of your opponent, you have an unobstructed view of the ball and the ball has an unobstructed path to the front wall. Your opponent has to maneuver around you at the very beginning of a well-placed kill shot to have any chance of recovering it and must therefore very early commit himself by moving closer to the front wall. Once such a commitment is made, an advanced player can change his shot, rendering the strategy of the defender useless. This explains why it is so important to move into center court early and not wait until your opponent begins to make his shot. If you are in the process of charging out of the back court, the opposing player can change from a kill to a low, hard pass shot down a side wall, which you would have little chance of returning.

There are several reasons for hitting a pass shot when in back of the other man. He must move swiftly laterally to return a low pass shot. If he elects to move into back court after the ball, you are left with center court. Also, he is less able to predict your moves when he is in front of you. At best, he can use only peripheral vision, since he dare not turn his head completely to watch you.

There are times, however, when your execution is poor, for example, when you hit a kill attempt far too high on the front wall and it comes back up court directly to the man in back of you. Since he then has all the options, you will have to watch him closely out of the corner of your eye. You may want to even move slightly to one side of the court to observe him better. In addition to giving you a better position of observation, you may help him decide to shoot into the larger part of the court. Move with the ball and if you have given him the right side of the court and you are right handed, you may have a fine opportunity for a kill with your strong hand.

Admittedly, this is dangerous strategy, but we are talking of situations demanding some maneuvering. A like situation may be encountered when you have made a poor serve into the right-hand corner to a right-hand player. Since you have given him a beautiful opportunity for a back-wall kill, why not ostentatiously edge a bit into left center court as soon as you have served and watch him carefully. As soon as the ball leaves his hand and you see it moving toward the right front wall, slide into right front court and go to work with your right hand. There are times when you can help your opponent select his shot to your advantage.

Of course, you are gambling whenever you yield a side of the court to the opposition. But there are occasions when you will have to gamble, either by rushing toward the probable point of the kill or toward the side of the probable pass shot. You may have to move during the swing but before the ball is hit, and you may guess wrong, but at least you will retrieve some hard-to-get shots. Even if you fail, you avoid that sick feeling that comes from being caught flat-footed.

Being caught flat-footed is perhaps the deadliest sin in handball. The game is highly mobile and to stand around invites disaster. For example, when you hit a ceiling ball too hard, move into center court quickly to guard against the possible back-wall kill which can be made from the rebound. Do not stand in back court watching the return of this easy-to-kill rebound.

Also use your mobility on serve returns. Do not position yourself a few feet from the center of the back wall and stolidly await the serve. If power serves are coming hard and low toward the right back corner and the server seems to dote on these, edge into the right side of the court. If the server switches tactics and lofts a high lob into the left rear corner, rush the ball and pound it down the left side wall, or hit it into the ceiling, or around the server in a fast, low pass shot. As we mentioned before, try rushing a few serves if the server does not seem to be watching you. If he constantly serves from one side of the court, hit the ball down the other side. He will lose the serve and his composure before he has time to move.

Try to move the server out of his center court position by occasional ceiling balls, around-the-wall shots, or pass shots hit off the serve. Do not attempt to force a handout by trying to kill every serve. If the server moves into the center court position immediately after the serve and is anticipating your return, killing the ball off the serve is not easy. And it should be repeated that, if the kill attempt is imperfect, the server will be in an excellent position to kill the ball himself. As the receiver, be mobile; do not position yourself too near the back wall or crowd into a corner.

Whether serving or receiving, once you have forced a weak return, especially one from deep back court, move up under it and fly kill it. You will sap your opponent's energy, since he must travel the length of the court to return your shot. Judicious use of this shot keeps the other man guessing and does not allow him to rest in back court.

The fly kill is also an excellent way to capitalize on weak service returns. The shot is made so quickly that the ball is often dead on the floor before the receiver can recover from his attempt to return the serve. Sometimes a kind of rhythm is generated: the server serves, the receiver returns, and the server fly kills the ball. The receiver must break that rhythm through ceiling, pass, or around-the-walls shots or the game is surely lost.

One way to break that rhythm and to cool off someone who is "hot" is to call a time out. The rules allow three time outs of 30 seconds each, and there is no better time to call a time out than when a player seems to be able to do nothing wrong. Many players garner points in streaks and, during these streaks, nothing you do seems to restrain them. To break their rhythm (and, not incidentally, to give you an opportunity to design countermeasures), you might call a time out, rest a bit, and do a little thinking. It might be that his string of points has you pressing a bit and that you are trying for kills off difficult serves or volleys. Try then to hit ceiling balls or around-the-walls shots and switch from back-wall kills to back-wall pass shots.

Defensive play like this must be stressed, for some players stubbornly persist in trying to kill the ball from awkward positions or while on the run. Learn defensive play and use it especially when your opponent seems to be holding center court and killing everything near him. Do not give him any-thing good to hit; that hoary old baseball maxim also applies to handball.

Your choice then is to be a thinking, watchful player or one who learns a few shots and relies on perfect execution of them. The latter will develop slowly and must break his accustomed pattern to become a successful player.

THE DOUBLES GAME

Position and teamwork are essential in doubles. To achieve this teamwork, each man must know the position of his partner in addition to those of the other two men. When these visual cues are added to following the flight of the ball, it is easy to see why there are more inputs to sort and act upon in doubles than in singles. Since the ball is hit more often in any given time period than in singles, doubles emphasizes speed and quick reactions. How-ever, since there are two men to cover the court, doubles requires less running and less total exertion.

Each member of a doubles team covers a part of the court (see Fig. 7-1 for the case of two right handers). The better of the two players—the one with the best left hand—takes the left side. He hits the majority of the shots since

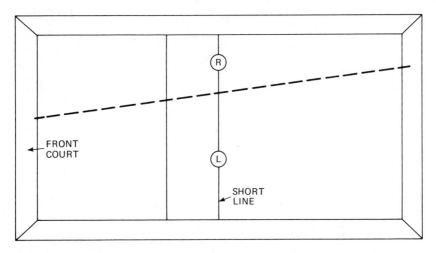

FIGURE 7-1. Dotted line through court shows approximate division of court responsibilities for a doubles team of two right handers. Circles diagram optimum front court position for same team.

he is in a position to take most of the shots that his partner on the right side would have to hit left handed. Many of these shots will be easy kills for the left man's strong hand.

There is one cardinal rule of doubles play: the player with the best shot at the ball takes it. In most cases, the player who most easily can get his strong hand on the ball makes the shot. Sometimes, however, the ball will rebound against the side wall next to a player in such a way that it is a difficult shot for that player. For example, the ball may hit the right side wall (see Fig. 7-2) close to the player on the right. Even though he theoretically can take the ball with his strong hand, he should let this shot through for his partner, who can position himself for a better shot. Of course, this teamwork takes two people observant enough to position themselves (drop back or move sideways or forward) correctly when they see their partner in trouble. In these instances, doubles is a noisier game than singles, for it is desirable to let your partner know that "you've got it," or to tell him to "take it" when you are in trouble. Talking back and forth helps avoid collisions and unnecessary running.

Collisions, however, are remarkably scarce in doubles when the players are experienced, mainly because the maneuvering for position is so disciplined. Both teams work for the coveted front court position, in which the player on the right stations himself about an arm's length away from the right wall and

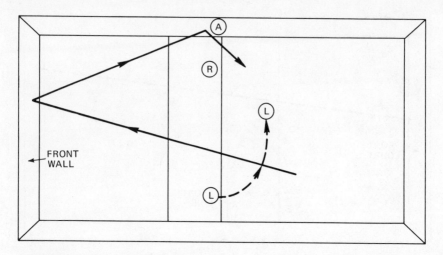

FIGURE 7-2. On a shot hitting the side wall at position A the man on the right (R) should let ball pass and his partner (L) should move (dotted line) to take ball. The reverse happens on left wall shot.

the player on the left stands closer to the center of the court. Both players (see Fig. 7-1) are very close to the short line, sometimes in back of it, and many times in front as the action becomes hectic.

This front court positioning is so important that it can be said of two doubles teams of roughly equal abilities that "the one consistently operating from the front court position will always win." The advantage of operating from the front court is that the team commanding this position can play more offensively than the team in back of them. The ball comes unobstructed, visually or physically, to the front court men, who then have the prime kill-shot opportunity. To guard against this kill-shot threat, the opposing team must move around or past the front court team. If an opposing team member makes his move too early, the man hitting the ball can change his shot with disastrous results for the opposition.

The team playing consistently in back court often cannot see the ball for a split second or so as it comes up court. This slight visual obstruction is not cause for a hinder, yet it can upset timing and create weak or missed returns.

Worse yet, the team unable to move into front court is forced into defensive handball, for they dare not attempt many kills from in back of an alert team. Since there are two men to cover the front court, any kill from the rear must be perfect or the rebound can be turned into a kill. Knowing this, the wise doubles team reverts to ceiling balls, pass shots, or around-the-walls shots to try and move one or both front court men out of their positions. This team should wait for a weak serve or volley shot before trying to put it away.

Serving is important, but, with two men waiting for the serve, aces are not as easily made in doubles as they are in singles. The server, therefore, should be content to work for weak returns. Two men who serve well enough to force weak returns and are well versed in fly killing make a formidable doubles team.

Although it is unwise to generalize about which serves are effective in doubles, the scotch toss or Z serve is one which often brings a weak return. It is more advantageous, however, to quickly try many serves to find the one most troublesome to the other team. Once this serve is known, use it often. Remember that this experimentation must be done for each team; each two-some has different strengths and weaknesses.

Once weaknesses are noted, be they in serving or volleying, exploit them. It may not be chivalrous, but it is permissible to work on the weak man. Hit the majority of the shots to him; after the other member of the team becomes sufficiently irritated, suddenly turn on him. By this time, he may be so mentally upset that he will miss shots he would normally kill.

After this counsel on how to introduce mental warfare to the courts, we should detail countermeasures. However, the only countermeasure lies in the ability of the individual to accept with grace this seeming injustice (working on the weak man). A player should also learn to accept occasional poor or below average performance in himself in singles. It is useless to become frustrated and to storm about the court, interrupting the game with loud exclamations. Such frustrations, once they begin to bite deeply, simply cause even poorer shots. The best way to avoid this is to shrug off a poor shot and concentrate on the reason for it to avoid repeating it.

Some tips to help doubles players are:

1. When your partner has a back-wall shot, move quickly in front of an opposing player to reduce the possibility of being hit by your partner's shot.

2. Immediately after your partner's serve passes the short line, get out of the server's box, turn toward the front, and prepare to volley. Do not let yourself be caught against the wall unable to return the ball.

3. If a man moves very close to the front wall to retrieve a kill, hit the ball into the front wall close to him on the chance that the rebound may hit him or that he will hurry or restrict his swing and miss the ball.

4. When playing a team composed of a left hander and a right hander, serve and drive low volley shots up the middle to exploit their offhand weakness.

5. If you see your partner in trouble and can help him by moving over into his side, call out and tell him "you've got it." It also helps to tell him to "let it go," if you see he is contemplating a very tough shot.

6. Beginners, do not place one man in front court and the other in back court. This does not work against any team with experience. No one man can cover the entire front court adequately, and, with two men in line, both often go for every side-wall shot and neither knows which one will handle the shot.

7. Finally, watch an experienced doubles team and put into practice what you learn from them. Better yet, challenge them to a match. You will progress in handball in conjunction with the caliber of your competition.

VERY BRIEFLY, YOU SHOULD NOW UNDERSTAND:

The importance of the center court position in both doubles and singles.

Why, in singles, you should generally pass shoot from in back of your opponent and kill when in front of him.

The advantages of finding the weaknesses of your opponent or opponents and emphasizing them.

The importance, in doubles, of communication between partners.

GLOSSARY

Ace: A legal serve the receiver is unable to return.

Angle Serve: See Z serve.

Anticipation: Art of predicting forthcoming shot and direction of rebound in order to move into best position to return the ball.

Back Court: Area of court extending from back wall to within about six feet of short line.

Back-wall Shot: Ball hit, usually with an underhand swing, as it rebounds from back wall.

Body Positioning: Stance and location of body on court relative to the ball.

Bolo Shot: A ball hit with the fist using short, underhand swing.

Bone Bruise: Deep, painful bruise on the hands near base of fingers, possibly caused by hitting the ball very hard after insufficient warm up.

Bottom Board: Portion of front wall next to floor against which unreturnable kill shots are hit.

Cardio-respiratory Endurance: The ability to continue strenuous physical activity.

Ceiling Serve: Ball hits ceiling after rebounding from front wall (a fault serve).

Ceiling Shot: Ball hit against ceiling near front wall to bring it in a high bounce down against back wall.

Center Court Position: Advantageous location in middle of court near short line which player should attempt to maintain.

Court Dimensions, Four-wall: 40′ X 20′ X 20′.

Crotch Ball: Shot striking junction of wall and floor.

Cutthroat: Three people play in rotation, the server playing the other two.

Doubles: Four men play in teams of two.

Eye Guard: Wire or plastic protective devices fitting around or over the eyes to prevent injury.

Fault Serves: Nonplayable serves (ceiling, short, long, two sides); two in succession constitute a handout.

Fist Shot: Ball hit with fist.

Fives: Early name for game of handball.

Fly Kill: Shot made by hitting ball in flight low into front wall or front corners.

Fly Volley: Hitting the ball in flight (before it bounces on floor).

Foot Fault: Act of stepping on or over service line or starting on or behind short line during the serve.

Front Court: Area of court extending from service line to front wall.

Gloves, Handball: Specially made padded or unpadded gloves of cowskin, goatskin, or deerskin.

Handout: Loss of serve.

Hinder: Act of visually or physically blocking the opposition from a clear shot at the ball.

Hop: Spin put on ball by combined wrist-hand action causing ball to change direction upon contact with floor.

Kill Shot: Ball hit low into front wall or front-wall corner.

Lob Serve: Softly hit ball traveling in a high arc along side wall or across court and dropping sharply into a back-wall corner.

Long Serve: Ball travels to back wall before contacting floor (a fault serve).

Midcourt: Area from about six feet in back of short line to service line.

Motor Learning: Process of acquiring a physical skill.

Offhand: Weak hand—left hand of natural right hander and vice versa.

Pass Shot: Hard shot usually driven down a side wall with the intent of moving the ball around opposition and into back court.

Power Serve: Ball is driven as fast and as low as possible, often with hop, toward a back-wall corner.

Scotch Toss Serve: See Z serve.

Screen Ball: Server or his partner unavoidably blocks opposition from seeing rebound of serve.

Serve: Player hits ball from between short and service lines against front wall so that it rebounds to the floor behind the short line and may be returned by the opposition.

Service Box: 18" wide boxes along both walls between short and service lines accommodating nonserving doubles partner while his partner is serving.

Singles: Two-man play.

Stroke: Compact, short swing of forearm and wrist characterizing proper handball form.

Terminator: Nonreturnable game point serve.

Trap Shot: Ball is struck with open hand immediately after it bounces on floor.

Two-side Serve: Rebound from front wall strikes both side walls before touching floor (a fault serve).

Volley: Exchange of shots following serve.

Volleying Rate: Frequency at which ball is hit.

Wrist Flexion: Snap or whip of wrist movement necessary to propel ball at high speed.

Wrist Shot: Ball hit on wrist; penalized by loss of serve or gain in point.

Z Serve: Ball hit sharply into front-wall corner, travels across court, strikes side wall, and bounces off parallel to back wall.

BIBLIOGRAPHY

Banister, E. W., *et al.* 1964. The caloric cost of playing handball. *Research Quarterly* 35:236-40.

Championship handball plus official handball rules. United States Handball Assn., 4101 Dempster Street, Skokie, Ill.

Griffith, M. A. 1960. *An objective method of evaluating ability in handball singles.* Columbus, Ohio: Ohio State University (unpublished M.A. thesis).

Holt, L. E. 1969. A comparative study of selected handball techniques. *Research Quarterly* 40:700-703.

Kendler, Robert. 1969. *ACE.* Skokie, Ill: United States Handball Assn.

Johnson, Perry B., *et al.*, 1966. *Physical education: a problem solving approach through health and fitness.* New York: Holt, Rinehart and Winston.

Mand, Charles L. 1968. *Handball fundamentals.* Columbus, Ohio: Charles E. Merrill Publishing Company.

Menke, F. G. 1969. *The encyclopedia of sports.* South Brunswick, N.J.: A. S. Barnes.

Montoye, H. J., Brotzman, J. 1951. An investigation of the validity of using the results of a doubles tournament as a measure of handball ability. *Research Quarterly* 22:214-18.

O'Connell, Charlie. 1964. *Handball illustrated.* New York: The Ronald Press Co.

Pennington, G. G., *et al.* 1967. A measure of handball ability. *Research Quarterly* 38:247-53.

Seyffarth, H. 1940. The behavior of motor units in voluntary contractions. *SKR. Worke Vidnsk Akad. I. Mat.-Nat Kl.* 4:17

Singer, R. N. 1968. *Motor learning and human performance: an application to physical education skills.* New York: The MacMillan Company.

Tumbull, L. M. 1964. *A comparison of the cardiorespiratory changes as determined by treadmill performance occurring in selected University of Washington males enrolled in the selected physical education activities.* Seattle, Wash.: University of Washington (unpublished M.S. thesis).

INDEX